Introductory Course

to

Images and Intentions

By

Duanita G. Eleniak, PhD

A must-read for everyone working in

the field of arts and healing

Other Books by the author:

The Role of the Arts in Shifting Consciousness

Program to Activate your Business Consciousness

Mini-Workbook for Program to Activate Your Business Consciousness

The Daily Business Intentions Journal

The Daily Intentions Journal

Inspiring Daily Business Intentions

Be the Change: Acting with Intention

Online Courses by the author:

Course in Daily Intentions

Introductory Course to Images and Intentions

Counselling Ethics and the New Worldview

Course in Forgiveness

Program to Activate your Business Consciousness

Counsellors and Private Practice: Business Series

Financial Freedom Study Group

Course Available at the American Art Therapy Association Career Center at
http://arttherapy.trainingcampus.net/uas/modules/trees/windex.aspx

Art Therapy with Street Youth

Acknowledgments

Special thanks to Kathryn, a wise Web woman without whom these electronic endeavors would remain a mystery to me; and to my editing and publishing team -- I appreciate your guidance. And to Eileen, editor extraordinaire who inspires me to put my work into the world.

Thank you to all my wonderful teachers and mentors over the years who have shared so much with me. I can only hope my work continues to honor yours.

Thank you to all my clients and students throughout the years who have taught me so much in our work together. You are the reason that I keep writing and sharing.

Thank you to my friends and my family who provide me with my balance.

And, as always, thanks to my lovely daughter Leila and my menagerie of animals that are my constant cheerleaders!

May this introduction be a helpful start for all of you interested in the area of images, intentions, and healing.

Table of Contents

Chapter 1: Introduction

Welcome to the *Introductory Course to Images and Intentions*.

Who Is This Course for?

This course is for anyone interested in learning how to work with images alongside intentions to manifest their reality and make changes in their life.

What Do I Need to Do This Course?

Supplies to do this course include a three ring binder with lined and plain paper; a variety of magazines that you can cut up for images; a pen; scissors (though if you are comfortable with ripping paper these are unnecessary); glue or double-sided tape; art materials if you would like to sketch, draw, or add to your collage (materials could range from crayons, felts, a small set of watercolor paints, etc.).

In Appendix II of this book you will find two sample pages for your daily intentions journal: copy them for your own journal. One is a journal page where you will write your intentions down every morning. The other is a page where you will create your images on a daily basis to reflect your intentions.

Where Do I Get Supplies?

Good places to get art supplies include: dollar stores; Chinatown; stores like Staples and Walmart; recycling bins for magazines and newspapers. Interesting tidbits can also be found in places that sell scrapbooking supplies.

What Areas Of My Life Can I Change?

You can work with intentions and images in any area of your life that you want to change: health; family; friends; intimate relationships; a new home; travel; etc. You can work with change on an outer level, as well as on an inner level regarding how you think, aspects of your character, virtues you would like to develop, etc.

What Kind of Time Commitment Is Required for This Course?

Take the time to review the initial material to the course. After that, the course will take about a half hour every morning for 40 days. During this time you will be doing two pages in your journal every morning. On one page you will write daily intentions and on the other you will make images to go with them. You can copy the format from the pages in Appendix II and create your own pages or download a ready-made journal from www.mentoringstore.ca.

Once you experience the power of working with intentions and images on a daily basis in your life, you may find that you wish to continue the practice. Fuelled by positive experiences, many students have continued to experiment with intentions and images for decades after this initial introductory course.

Vision Boards and Vision Journals

Working with daily intentions and images is kind of like making mini vision boards every day. Vision boards are often larger pieces which require more time to make. Another common term for the book you use when working with intentions and images is a "visual journal." All this means is that you have a record of your intentions in image form over time. No matter by what name, all these ways of working with images are based on the same principles.

Chapter 2: Seven Advantages in Working with Images and Intentions

Working with images and intentions together is a powerful way to magnify the ability of your intention to magnetize a new reality that includes the changes that you want to make in your life. It has several advantages over working just with words and intentions.

Advantage One: Holding Your Attention throughout the Day

One of the most frequent complaints from people who work with only word and intention is that they do their intention in the morning, magnetize it and then by the middle of the day they have trouble remembering what their intention of the day is. Sometimes they go through their entire day and forget that they are doing daily intentions at all.

When you are working with images, however, your constant search for new pictures can help you to focus on your daily intentions and remember them. The extra attention can serve as a magnifying effect on your attention.

Advantage Two: Holding the Intention

An image can hold the intentions in visual form which, when placed in places where you can see them daily allow levels of your consciousness to remain in constant awareness of your intended realities. Once again this magnifies the intent by holding it at some level of consciousness.

Advantage Three: A Picture Is Worth a Thousand Words

Working with images can be a quick and easy way to establish a feeling that might take thousands of words and a lot of time to describe.

Advantage Four: The Brain Works in Images

When you work with images rather than words you are actually using the language of the brain which works in symbols. The levels of consciousness to which we are appealing for the miracles involved in shifting realities have, as their first language, symbols and images rather than words. You can just think about your dreams to understand this point.

Advantage Five: Images Allow for Ease of Review over Time

A visual record of your intentions is easier to review over time than thousands of words. A quick glance at pictures can allow you to notice whether or not an intention from the past has come to fruition.

Advantage Six: Images Elicit Feelings Inherently

Because the world of aesthetics enters in when you are working with images, the ability to elicit feelings can happen through conscious as well as unconscious ways through line, shape, and form.

Advantage Seven: Working with Photographs

Working with photographs that are printed off or photocopied is a powerful way to picture yourself in new realities. The feelings elicited when you see yourself in your new home, new relationship, and/or new body shape help you to imagine how the world would look if the reality was happening now.

Chapter 3: Begin with Commitment

The best way to do this course is to begin with an active commitment which will allow you to participate in daily actions long enough to connect with your power to change your life.

Below you will find an example of a commitment. Write out the commitment, sign it, and put it in a place where you can see it and where it can serve as a reminder for you to take the daily actions necessary to attract new realities into your life.

Does the written commitment need any changes to better suit your personal goals? If so, make the necessary changes before you sign it. Then post it.

Commitment

I, _____, do hereby commit to doing daily work with images and intentions for a period of 40 days.

I commit to waking up a half hour early every day. I commit to writing an intention for the day and then creating an image to go with the intention.

I commit to self-care during this period of time. I eat well, I drink plenty of water, I get enough rest and I exercise.

I commit to an attitude of open-mindedness as I do the work. I am willing to simply do the work and learn from my adventures.

I do this daily work with the intention that I learn the ways of co-creation in partnership with Creative Source Energy.

Signature: _____

Date: _____

Chapter 4: Dealing with External Resistance Factors

One of the first things to address when doing a course like this is resistance to change. Resistance to changing your reality can come from outside influences in your life or from inside yourself. In this section we will address how to deal with external resistance factors.

If you discover that you are hesitant to begin the work or that you have not done your daily intention work for several days, you may be dealing with external resistance factors; things that happen outside your realm of control that make you question what you are doing. They work against your commitment to do the daily work.

External Factors Creating Resistance to Change

1. **People:** One of the most common external factors that create resistance to change is people in your life who fail to support you. If there is someone in your environment who is critical, skeptical, or ridicules your desire and/or ability to change your life, protect yourself. Keep your work hidden and protected from him or her.

   A special locking journal or a drawer to put away your daily work may suffice. Some students do their daily writing and images and then immediately shred it. They do this to stop their inner censors. Others protect their work from being read by others who may not believe in their abilities to connect with life-changing forces. In this way they can allow themselves to dream fully on the page, knowing no one will ever see it.

2. **Environment:** Sometimes your environment means that you cannot trust that your journal will remain safe. Perhaps you live in a basement suite with no room for a vision board.

   In this case, you could make your vision board small, or even digital, and keep it safe and hidden away this way.

3. **Travel and sleepovers:** Many students have a difficult time honoring their daily commitment to living life intentionally when traveling or sleeping away from home. They found several ways to keep the process going, and discovered that being on holiday or away from home is in fact the perfect time to write and create images. The chance of being more able to tap in imaginally is amplified during these times.

   - **The right attitude:** Think of doing your daily intentions like brushing your teeth. You brush your teeth daily to ensure oral health. You write and create your daily intentions to ensure emotional health. Just as you do your very best to remember your toothbrush, do your very best to remember your intentions journal.
   - **Downsizing the book:** Students who were traveling found it easiest to do their daily intentions in a small book that was light and easy to carry. When traveling, get a small notebook and make mini images. Never let the fact that you are going on vacation affect your work!

Since it is the **feeling** generated while doing this work that is critical to the manifestation process, even if you cannot keep the physical form of your work, your intentions are still being activated and received by a responsive Universe.

Are there any external barriers to change that you can anticipate? If so, what can you do to protect your work and allow yourself the chance to change?

Chapter 5: Dealing with Internal Resistance Factors

Internal Factors Creating Resistance to Change

A majority of people go into a tailspin of resistance as soon as the words "art," "art materials," or "creative" are mentioned. Old wounds and the lack of acknowledgment of the fact that creativity is a natural right for all people often creates fear for students around doing activities that involve making things.

It is crucial for you to recognize as soon as possible that your fear is simple resistance that you can shift. The voices come from an inner part of you that may have been hurt, is scared, and will keep you from going forward with your learning unless you become aware of this part and take action to heal very quickly.

Common Excuses to Check for

1. **"I can't do the course. I am not an artist. I'm not creative."** You actually have an advantage if you are not an artist and are untrained artistically. Your lack of control over the finished product will allow a greater chance for "creative accidents" to happen. We will discuss these in greater detail in the next section.

2. **"I have no place to set up a workstation."** To do with care, all you need is paper and a pen. No workstation is necessary to begin.

3. **"I have no money."** The money excuse is ranked as one of the top excuses for failing to pursue inner promptings to connect with your creative power and do something to begin changing your life. Just a writing utensil and any form of paper is all you need to do this course. There is no need for fancy art materials or journals. In fact, the simpler the materials the better, especially if you are a person who does not like to "mess up" beautiful new journals or art material.

4. **"I have no time"** or **"I am not a morning person."** I have seen morning intentions and images done in five minutes in the bathroom while getting ready to go to work. Bathrooms can be perfect places to catch five minutes away from children or a busy lifestyle. If you commit to simply doing the process, you will find the time, even in the morning.

5. **"I have no good ideas for intentions. I don't know what to write."** This is where working in community with other like-minded people comes in handy. When you listen to what other people are working on, how they are wording their intentions, and how they are making them happen, your own ideas will be sparked and your imagination will take over.

For specific ideas about intentions connected to business and work go to the bookstore at www.mentoringstore.ca/books.html and find the book *Inspiring Daily Business Intentions* (Eleniak, 2010).

The "'Yeahbut" Loop

Be aware of the "yeahbut" loop and if you catch yourself doing it, immediately recognize the fact that part of you is being resistant to change.

The "yeahbut" loop happens when you make an excuse every time someone suggests you do something that allows your intentions to come into reality. For example, you say "I have no time in the morning to do my intentions and images"" to which your partner replies, "Well, I can get up in the morning with the children, so you have time," to which you reply, **"Yeah, but** I have to make the lunches in the morning." Your supportive partner then says, "Well, let's make them before we go to sleep," to which you reply, **"Yeah, but** I have to call Suzie in the mornings and arrange to pick up her children for school," to which your supportive partner says "I can make arrangements with Suzie or we can do it the night before," and again you reply, **"Yeah, but** … " This is an example of a "yeahbut" loop which is an indicator that some form of resistance is going on.

If you find yourself in a "yeahbut" loop ask yourself, "What am I afraid of?" and "How badly do I want to change my reality?"

Blurts

"Blurts" are negative self-talk from our inner critic that can pop up from time to time as we work with images. "Blurt" is a word coined by Julia Cameron in her book *The Artist's Way: A Spiritual Path to Higher Creativity.*

As you work with your daily images you may become aware of a voice in your head which says things like: "What are you doing? Playing like a kid. And this is supposed to change your life? Who are you kidding anyway? You are so gullible. You are just wasting your time. You aren't even any good at doing this. Everyone else's pictures are so much better than yours. You never were creative."

Sound familiar? Blurts are based in old negative belief systems about yourself and how life works. Their sole purpose is to prevent change and disempower you. This part of yourself may honestly think that it is saving you by keeping you in a life which is the same. There is often a sense of safety in the reality that we know. Change can sometimes be disruptive.

What blurts run through your mind? Take a moment to write them down.

Dealing with Blurts

When you discover a blurt as you work, take a moment to draw a circle and write down the blurt inside of it. Imagine that the circle is a toxic waste container and the negative self-talk is the toxic waste that needs to be contained so that you are free to keep allowing yourself to explore with images.

Later, rewrite the blurt as an affirmative intention and make a collage image around it. For example, if your blurt is "You are not creative", catch the blurt and put it in a toxic container circle. Now rewrite the negative statement into an affirmation, for example, "I am very creative and the more I do the work the more I discover how creative I truly am." Now use pictures to show this new affirmative thought.

If you still find yourself resisting this affirmation or not believing it, rewrite it again until you find an affirmation which rings true for you. For example, you could rewrite the affirmation to, "I fully intend on connecting with my creativity and with the Creative Power that flows through me assisting changes in my life to happen."

Carefully record all blurts that happen at each stage of your creative process working with affirmative intentions and images. Work with the process described above as often as you need to with each negative statement that you discover you have.

What you will notice over time is that the negative self-talk gets less frequent and less intense over time. The negative statements are kind of like weeds. You need to very patiently become aware of them, and one by one pull them out. The ones with a deep root system or that have many seeds might take a longer time to remove from your newly discovered fertile ground of creativity. With patience and perseverance, however, you will reclaim your creative ground and your connection to Creative Source Energy. You will reconnect with your positive power to create the life of your dreams.

Take the blurts that you identified, rewrite them as affirmative intentions and make a collage to go with each of the shifts in thought to which you aspire.

How Do You Move Out of Resistance?

If you find part of yourself resistant or scared to do the daily images and intentions simply:

1. Recognize that it is only a part of yourself that is resistant rather than your whole self. There is a bigger part of you that does want to work with images which is why you find yourself even reading about initial resistance.

2. Recognize that the resistant part of you is simply afraid. Very often this is a creative part of you that has been very hurt in the past. See if you can recognize the inner voice that is attempting to prevent you from working creatively with images. Is there anyone in the past who told you, "You can't draw" or "It's your sister that is the artist, not you"? Has anyone ridiculed or criticized your creative endeavors in the past? If you can recognize a creative injury that you sustained, take a moment to write down your experience. Can you forgive the bully from your past and release yourself to experience your creative self now?

3. When dealing with an inner critic that wants to stop you from expressing yourself in images, imagine talking to this part of yourself and say, "Thank you for sharing. I appreciate that you think you are trying to help me. I would like to experience making these images anyhow." Give yourself permission to go ahead and take the next step. Bring out your art materials. Look through the magazines for images. Glue something to a page. Let yourself do it anyhow.

Chapter 6: Introduction to the Range of Medium

Different art media by their very nature will allow you increased or decreased control of the effect of the image on an emotional level. Being aware of this range of control and the impact on you at a level of feeling can assist you to choose a medium or mediums to enhance the purpose of your intention. It is the **feelings** experienced in the work of manifesting that cause the vibrations that attract new realities into physical form. Keep this in mind when creating your images.

Please remember that the statements about medium below are generalities based on most people's experiences. There will always be exceptions to the generalities depending on training of individuals, past experiences with art materials, etc.

The most important point to get out of the explanation of the continuum of control inherent in medium, is that if you work with art materials intentionally, it is possible that you can vary the effects of your intentions and images.

Black and White versus Color

In general, working in color elicits more of an emotional response to the image than black and white. If you want to experience more feelings, work in color. If you want to control the intensity of feeling, see what happens if you work in black and white.

Lighter Colors versus Darker Colors

In general, the darker the color the more feelings are elicited.

Bigger Images versus Smaller Images

In general, the bigger an image is the more impact it will have on a level of feeling for people. If you want to amplify the effect of one of your intentions or images, see what happens if you use bigger paper.

A Word on Shape

We have become very accustomed to our paper being given to us in rectangular shape. Give the shape of your paper some thought. What happens if you use a triangle for your paper or to outline the image that you draw on it? The power of triangles has long been noted, for example, in the design of the great pyramids. Think also about working in circles. Circles are archetypes which occur naturally and which have been used for healing purposes in mandalas, magic circles, and medicine wheels. Remember to experiment with shapes to bring power consciously to your images in alignment with your intentions.

A Word on Speed

Every once in a while, consciously challenge yourself to complete your image in a very small amount of time. Having to work quickly can help you bypass conscious control over the end product and can facilitate the occurrence of "creative accidents," which can bring our attention to areas of need. At other times, consciously allow yourself longer times to work on your images. Slowing down can prompt imagination and daydreams which could prove to be essential to your creative manifesting process.

White Paper versus Colored versus Recycled

Consider the base of your image, the paper. Give thought to the color of the paper with which you want to work. Do different colors have different associations for you? If you used a particular color for the background of your image might it elicit your feelings in a different way than simply doing the image on white paper? How could you amplify the feeling that you need to make your intention as powerful as it can be on a vibrational level?

Think about using a newspaper or a full magazine page as the base of your image. How can the background inform the image that you create on top? Are there any interesting coincidences that happen in the relationships between the base and what you create on top?

Glue versus Glue Sticks versus Double-Sided Tape

Glue sticks are probably the most popular way to work with pictures to make collages because they are highly portable, easy to use, and they are usually mess-free. Liquid glue can get messy. Double-sided tape is a great option if you are creating an image and might like to change parts of it later; that is, if you want to have the freedom to move things around and make changes.

Types of Media

Art materials that you can use to create your images will provide you a continuum of control regarding intensity of feelings experienced. In general, going from the most control to the least control, the types of materials you can use include:

1. **Pencils:** These provide a high degree of control especially when used in combination with an eraser and/or compass set.

2. **Charcoal sticks:** While the black and white nature of charcoal generally elicits less of an emotional response, the relative softness of the medium and the ability to smudge it gives it the potential for more expression of feeling than pencils.

3. **Pencil crayons:** This movement into color gives you the control of the pencil and a bit more potential to elicit feeling due to the color.

4. **Wax crayons:** The softness of wax crayons, the smell, the color, and the fact that you may have used them as children usually give wax crayons a higher ability than pencil crayons to elicit a response from us.

5. **Chalk and/or soft pastels:** The color and the softness of the medium allows for more potential feeling, however the relative softness of the colors mediates this.

6. **Watercolor pencils:** These give the combination of the relative control of the pencil crayon with the possibility to move into the more watery world of paint if water is applied. This medium can be considered a crossover medium to the increasing fluidity of feeling that happens in the world of paint.

7. **Felt pens:** The boldness of color possible with felt pens offers an opportunity for bright feelings while the exacting nature of the pen allows for control. There is relatively no ability to change intensities of feeling as there is with a pencil crayon which can be pushed on harder to get more intense feelings.

8. **Paint (finger paint; watercolors; acrylic; oil; oil sticks; water soluble oil):** The fluidity of paint, the relative intensity of color, and the fact that it is often applied with a brush or other utensil generally makes it a medium that can elicit a lot of feelings.

9. **Three-dimensional medium (clay, Plasticine, Play-Doh, sculpture, wax):** Any of the media which take an image from two dimensions to three have the ability to also bring forth a whole new dimension of feeling into the reality of the experience. Once again, size, color, and shape are considerations regarding what kind of feelings are actually elicited and their intensity.

10. **Collage:** Collage is one of the most highly recommended mediums to use if you are just beginning your work with intentions and images. The most important reason for this is that it allows you to work with already formed images which cut through the "I am not an artist" block very easily and simply. It also gives you a high degree of control over the final image, usually results in an image which can avoid an inners critic's harsh gaze, and can allow you to express what you want even if you have no technical skill with art materials. It is simple, quick, highly portable, and effective.

Chapter 7: Tips on Working with Collage

To Rip or Not to Rip

A frequent block for people just beginning to collage their images is resistance to ripping or cutting up magazines. You will hear, "I hate ripping up magazines. I can't use a National Geographic for that!"

 To get through this block:

> 1. "Save" magazines from recycling bins. Tell yourself that they were going to "die" anyway. With you creating images from them at least they will go to their graves with purpose.
>
> 2. Convince yourself that the beautiful magazines are being transformed rather than destroyed and that they are being transformed in an act of serving the world for a Higher Purpose.

A Wide Variety of Magazines

Ensure that you collect magazines representing a wide variety of subject areas (travel, home, garden, bridal, psychology, sports, cooking, etc.), and those targeted to various ethnic groups (Caucasian, East Indian, Aboriginal), etc. If you do not have such a variety begin collecting magazines from recycling bins.

Collect Your Collage Images

Once you discover the power of images in communicating intentions and incorporate this activity as a routine to your days, you will want to be on the constant lookout for images to collect. Can you rip that page out of the old magazine in your doctor's office? Can you keep that business card with the interesting logo? Can you rip that word or that picture out of the newspaper? Gee, that mail advertisement has a beautiful picture. Do you think you might use it one day? Perhaps you'll save old greeting cards, or specific images printed from the computer, or photocopied photos.

Collect images to work with in your intentional collage anywhere and everywhere you encounter them. Having your eyes open to collecting powerful images throughout your day helps keep your work with intentions in constant focus. This is a highly significant advantage that working with images and intentions has over working only with words and intentions. We know that whatever we place our attention on will amplify. The more we can focus on our intentions, the images, and the feelings that they elicit, the more powerfully we magnify the attraction of our desired reality.

Work with Photographs

Printing off or photocopying photographs as pictures for your intentions can be a powerful way to literally put yourself into the picture of new realities. Literally seeing yourself in collaged images of your new home or your new relationship or in the new body shape that you are working toward is a powerful way to evoke feelings that allow you to imagine the reality as if it were happening now.

Store Your Collage Images

Make your storage of images suit your lifestyle. If you are highly mobile, consider cutting out images and putting them in a big envelope that can go with you. Some people like a folder with different sections so that they can categorize images for quick retrieval.

For those of you who work in the same location each time you do your daily intentions, consider making a little workspace which holds your images and your supplies. You may even be able to have a stack of magazines there since portability is a non-issue. Containers are another thing you could employ to hold the pictures and supplies you use for your intention images.

Chapter 8: A Word about Creative Accidents

"Creative accidents" are things that happen when working with art materials that lead to exploration in areas that you may have never thought you would explore. When they happen it is as if a wiser part of yourself wants to bring your attention to something, and in the end, it is as if you can explain something that you may or may not have set out to explain in the beginning.

Being untrained artistically can actually be an advantage when working with images and intentions because having less training means you have less control over the medium. Having less control means that there is more of a chance for something "other" to come through on the page.

You can specifically choose art materials to work with for their inherent ability to increase or decrease the possibility of having a "creative accident."

Examples of "Creative Accidents"

Example one

You decide to use paints to make an image of your intention. As you are working, accidentally a drop of red paint drips on the page and suddenly the person in your picture is bleeding. What looks like a blood spot has landed right on the place in the body where you were hurt in a car accident at three years old. Though you did not mean to, the creative accident, if followed, allows for attention to the trauma that you experienced at the time and the resulting fear that you continue to hold today in your body.

Example two

You are ripping out pictures for collage and you cut out a page for the image on one side of the paper. As you are working you have an accident and your whole pile of images falls to the floor. As you pick up the mess you see the other side of the page you pulled and a word jumps out at you that is very meaningful. You use the word in your intention image and it takes you to a whole new place of consideration and meaning.

Example three

You have decided to take one of your daily images and make it three-dimensional using clay. Despite taking much care crafting the piece and placing it in the kiln, while it is being fired it explodes. It is the piece you did on letting go of your first marriage. The clay exploding is like a sign to you that the transformation is complete and that you do not have to keep reminders of it around any longer. Even on a literal level the piece is transformed to bits.

Example four

You are drawing a picture of your family. You finish up and you realize you've unintentionally left out an important family member. Or, you finish up and realize one family member is taking up a disproportionate amount of space. Could this be pointing out something you've been avoiding, or something you didn't realize until now?

Example five

You create a collage that deals with an emotional memory you wish you could purge, and, not realizing some glue had gotten underneath it and glued it to the table, you try to move it and it tears in half. It feels good. The ripping in half of the image symbolizes letting go of the bad memory.

Chapter 9: Honoring Images and the Creative Process

Images have a life of their own once they are created. They are like having children. They come through us. We fool ourselves into thinking that they are ours, but they are independent of us.

Images have a life force of their own. They are powerful forces that magnetize and can change and impact anyone who observes them simply through their nonverbal aesthetic, their line, shape, and form. There have been some art therapists who have gone so far as to write about how images are angels.

If we can appreciate that our images have a life of their own then it becomes important to regard them well. We must take care in how we handle them, how we speak about them, who we show them to, and who we protect them from.

An image has a life force and a creative spirit moving through it. If you regard it with the same dignity that you would regard another person, you will be doing well.

Containment or Protection of Images

Sometimes it is important to contain very important images of intentions. There are several ways to do this:

1. **Borders or frames:** Sometimes if an image of an intention is very special to you, putting a frame around it can help emphasize this. You can make a frame from paper, draw a frame around the picture, or work with framing material to literally frame it.

2. **Sealing images:** To seal an image of an intention you can buy liquids to paint over collages to hold the pictures securely over time. Some people use a thin coat of white glue for this purpose. Others put their images under glass or in plastic for protective purposes.

3. **Double frames:** Drawing multiple frames or putting multiple frame pieces around an image can be a way to physically protect a special intention throughout time.

4. **Taking pictures of images:** Taking pictures of your images is a good way to keep a visual record over a long period of time. This is especially true for people who have limited storage space for physical books.

Honoring the Creative Process

When you are creating images of intentions you are engaged in a creative process and tapping into Creative Source Energy. This is the same energy that makes the grass grow, your nails grow, and your hair grow. It is a creative energy and life force that animates and brings new creations to life.

As such, it is wise to honor your process. Just as you would not uncover grass seeds to show others that you have planted grass, sometimes your seedling images of new realities need to be kept quiet so that they are given a chance to grow. Sometimes exposure to the light, or talking about them too soon or to the wrong people can serve to stop their process. This is especially true if shown to people who discredit or make fun of your process. Protect your images as if they were seeds that you were planting in a fertile Universe that can grow them over time, and sometimes even underground in places where we cannot observe what is happening.

Chapter 10: Image Intention Reviews: Watching for Change over Time

It is highly recommended that you do a visual review of all of your daily images at least once a month (if you are working with intentions daily) or once every six months to a year if you are working less frequently.

To do an image review, take all of the images that you have done over the past month (or time period you choose) and put them up on the wall in chronological sequence. Look at them and check for the following:

Manifestations

Check to see if any of the images have come through to physical reality. Because manifestation into physical form can take time, sometimes we forget what we asked for. The form may already be in your physical world and it is helpful to review your images to watch for the manifestations. There is no feeling like it when you spot a match. These discoveries go a long way to helping you continue the process of daily intentions even through the "dry spells" if you feel you are ineffective as a manifestor. These sightings help to bring renewed faith to the process because they provide unarguable proof beyond any doubt that the process works.

Themes

Check for themes in your work. Are you asking for the same thing more than once? Do you have a color or image theme going? Do you have a preponderance of images in any one area of life?

Recurring Images

Watch for recurring images and patterns in your work. Note all the places that the same image, color, or shape occurs. Note any changes in these areas that have happened over time.

Shifts of Focus

What is usually in the very middle of your images? What do you place at the center of attention in your images? Does this focus vary? Do the intentions that you are working with vary over time? If so, how has your focus shifted?

It is helpful if you can find a friend or several friends that believe in you and your process to look at the pictures with you. Sometimes fresh eyes spot things that yours no longer see.

Make notes of what you have observed by doing this visual review over time. Keep the notes in a separate book that you can pull out next time you get together with your supportive friends to review your intentions over time.

Chapter 11: On the Importance of Feedback from Your Images

Ensure that you remember to put the images of your intentions up in places where you will see them daily. This provides a feedback loop for your brain which keeps the images and the intentions alive and activated long after your conscious mind has forgotten that it is there.

Being able to hold intentions alive in your brain and body over time is a highly effective way of keeping them activated and vibrating in realms which allow the attraction of the form into physical reality.

Active Imagination

In addition to visual feedback you can ask your images for direct feedback through your imagination (the images are alive and have a life of their own, remember?). Yes, I am asking you to talk to your images, listen to them, and hold a conversation with them. Dr. Carl Jung, a psychologist, called this "active imagination."

I also recommend recording the conversations in writing (or in audio) so that you can reflect on them.

Some people experiment with using different hands for the characters/images that they are conversing with and themselves. The reason for this is that your dominant hand becomes the hand your voice comes through. Because it is more difficult to write or draw with your non-dominant hand, forcing yourself to use it will make you slow down and your thoughts will need to slow down too. As your mind is quieted, it will be easier to "hear" what the image has to say.

As soon as you "hear" it, stop what you're doing and start writing down what you hear the image telling you. Once you have finished listening to and writing down the voice of the image, you can respond by writing down your response, still with your non-dominant hand. Continue this process until you feel it is complete. Notice how the imagined feedback from the images makes you feel.

Chapter 12: The Power of the Collective: Community Is Important

The power of the collective has been well documented in the cases of group meditations, prayers, and intention. You can harness this energy while doing work with images and intentions.

Let people that you trust know your intentions. Ask your trusted friends to put your intentions and images into their prayer or intention groups.

Do intentions for your family with your family.

Form intention pods, tribes, creative clusters, or support groups.

Check out the *Course in Daily Intentions* at MentoringStore.ca to find like-minded individuals working with the same tools as you on a daily basis.

There are a wide variety of ways that you can get together with other people to intensify the power of your images and intentions. Create community and work with others to change your reality.

Remember, you can always imagine your very best community ever and work with them as images on the imaginal level -- like an active imagination.

Whether you work with an outer, physical community or an inner, non-physical community (or both), keep the feeling of being lifted by other like-minded people with you always.

Chapter 13: Acceptance: Sometimes the Universe Has Other Plans

Creative ideas, new realities, and change often need periods of incubation where they are imagined, activated, and left to be until they come out in their own time (or not).

Just like with any kind of pregnancy that brings new life and realties to form, we enter an arena that is beyond our control when we work with manifesting intentions through images. Just like in a pregnancy, we take the necessary actions to bring our vision to conception. Whether or not the activation ignites forces beyond our control, imbeds in fertile ground if it does ignite, and whether or not it continues to term and to an actualized life in our physical reality is an area that is beyond our control. Here we enter the arena of Creative Source Energy and where we require action on behalf of a responsive Universal Creative Energy.

When doing this work, it is crucial to practice acceptance:

I accept that there are mysteries in my reality.

I accept that I can engage with and be in relationship with these mysteries.

I accept that there may be areas in life which are beyond my control.

I accept the wisdom inherent in forces larger than myself.

As humans, we can still only guess the degree to which we consciously control our reality and the degree to which our reality may be "fated." As we work with intentions consciously in relationship with Creative Source Energy we all move forward as pioneers exploring these edges of knowing.

Appendix I: Tips for Writing Effective Intentions

1. Affirm only what you want:

Think of and write about what **_you want._** The most common error people make when writing intentions is that they list everything that they *don't* want rather than focusing on what they **want**.

For example:

"I no longer have debt" is an affirmation which still includes a focus on "debt" in your reality. Substitute such affirmations with what you *do* want, for example, "I owe nothing and I am financially free."

2. Write "as if" it is happening _NOW_:

The second most common error people make is that they write their affirmation/intention in **future tense**, for example, "I will be going to New York," or "Money will come." This way of writing keeps your intention in the future.

Instead, write as if the intention is happening **NOW**, for example, "I **am in** New York"; "My money is here. I have more than enough money in my bank accounts."

3. Avoid using the words "don't", "can't", "not":

The levels of consciousness you are working with tend to bypass the negative tense. Reframe your affirmation into something that you **can** do and that you **do** want. For example, when you write "Today I don't think about a pink elephant" your mind skips the "don't" and you are already thinking of a pink elephant. You are more effective if you write what you **are** thinking about that day to assist the manifestation process.

4. Check for the words "try" and "but":

If you use the words "try" and "but" in affirmations ensure that this is actually what you want to do. "Try" is a very different verb than "do" in that you never **_accomplish_** what you want and you never **_do it_**, you simply **try**. You are always in process of "trying" to get what you want. For example, the affirmation "I try to write my journal pages every day" is very different than "I write my journal pages every day."

"But" is another word to be cautious with because it is a conjunction which wipes out everything in the sentence that you have written that comes before it. Ensure that this is what you **want** to do when you catch yourself using the word "but". For example, the affirmation "Today I spend at least 40 minutes managing my money but first I make my calls" only affirms that the writer will make their calls. The first part of the affirmation is "butted" away.

5. Begin with appreciation:

You can increase the power of your stated intention by beginning with appreciation "I am appreciative of …."

and then stating your intention. Appreciation is a very high vibrational frequency feeling and is responded to and reflected in a positive sense.

6. Make it believable:

Start with where you are and make your intention believable to you. When your intention still feels unreal to you it may be helpful to begin with "I am willing to ... " or "My intention is to ... ". For example, if it is your intention to be financially free and you are starting from a place of having nothing, writing "I am financially free" may feel untrue and you may feel disconnected from such a reality. In such a situation, find an affirmation which you have a positive feeling connection with, for example, "I fully intend on being financially free quickly and easily."

7. Deal immediately with "blurts":

Carefully note "blurts" and rewrite them as affirmative statements. Julia Cameron in her book, *The Artist's Way*, describes "blurts" as negative self-talk that may pop into your head when you are writing your daily journal. Their purpose is to stop you from change. They are based on old belief systems you have which need to be changed if you are to open to new possibilities and unlimited potential.

When you have "blurts" begin by becoming aware of them and then telling that part of yourself, "Thank you for sharing." Next, draw a circle in the margin of your journal page and write down the blurt in the circle. Finally, take the time to re-write the blurt as a positive affirmation or intention.

For example, you write your intention "I am a wildly successful soulful entrepreneur whose business sells products like hotcakes!" Inside your head you hear a part of yourself say, "Sure you are. You sold so much you don't even have enough money for that bill sitting on your table." That is a blurt. It is a negative inner voice who wants you to be "realistic" and knows that you will "never amount to anything more than what you are so why bother."

It is extremely important to catch these negative belief systems and make them obvious by writing them down inside the circle that you draw. Treat them like they are toxic waste and imagine that the circle you draw is a toxic waste container built to contain the poison. Once you can see them ask yourself, "Is this thought helpful? Will this thought get me to where I want to go?" and finally, "Do I want to change it?" If so, go and rewrite your affirmation in a way that can satisfy the inner critic and change its belief at the same time.

The original intention might now be: "I am grateful that I fully intend to be a wildly successful soulful entrepreneur whose business sells products and services like hotcakes!"

Once again on the rewrite, carefully and continually monitor for blurts as you write. If you hear more inner blurts repeat the process described until that inner critic part of you on the inside is satisfied and you can *feel good* about your intention.

8. Focus on the "feeling":

Write your intentions until you get the *"feeling"* of the daily statement. Mark Braden is one of the many scientists who notes that it is actually the vibrations caused by your *feelings* that attract new realities on a quantum level. Adding more and more detail in your writing about what your affirmation would **feel** "as if" it is happening right now tends to accomplish this.

For example, your intention might be "I practice self-care in my life."

Now keep writing and imagine how your life would be **if** this intention was fully operative right **NOW**. For example you might write: "I consciously work at economic self-care in order that I am able to take holidays, get regular massages, and practice self-care so that I always operate at the highest level of my potential." Keep writing connected ideas until you get a **feeling** of the intention operational. The more details you write the more you can get the *feeling* of how your life would be **if** the intentions were current reality. The more you get *the feeling*, the more powerful and magnetic your intentions become.

9. Ensure integrity:

If your daily intentions involve other people directly you must take caution to ensure that you align with the highest of integrity when you write them. If you are unsure of the effect on others of your daily affirmation it is highly recommended that before your intention you write, "If it is in the highest interests of all involved/concerned ... " One always wants to practice with the highest of integrity at these energetic levels of relationship and connection.

For example a counselor in business many want to put out a business intention requesting funding to be able to continue a woman's group that she is running. She might write the intention "Funding comes in and the group can keep going." But how do we know for sure that the group is meant to continue? Maybe it is meant to end and the group members meant to move on. In cases like this where you are unclear on motive, simply adding a preface to the intention like "If it is in the highest interests of all involved ... " can help prevent messing with any possible plans destiny might hold for others. Her affirmation might look like this: "If it is in the highest interests of all involved, funding comes in and the group keeps going."

10. Lastly remember:

Be careful what you ask for; you just might get it.

Appendix II: Blank Daily Intentions Journal Pages

We Co-Create our Day

Day Number: _____

Greeting/Invocation: _____

Daily intention:

_____

_____

_

Request for response:

_____

_____

Positive evidences experienced (signs, synchronicities, serendipities):

_____

_____

Appreciation:

_____

_____

_____

_____

Image of Daily Intention

_____

Appendix III: Resources

Supplemental resources available at www.mentoringstore.ca:

The free *Course on Daily Intentions* is available for you if you get blocked in your process and need further instruction.

Readymade journals at the bookstore: *The Daily Intentions Journal* (Eleniak, 2010), *The Daily Intentions Journal for Artists* (Eleniak, 2010) and *The Daily Business Intentions Journal* (Eleniak, 2010). All of these were journals written to be compatible with this course.

Membership in a community of people who are also experimenting with work in images and intentions is available as *Course in Daily Intentions Seminar.*

Program to Activate your Business Consciousness (course and workbook) is helpful if you would like to pursue working with intentions and images specifically to make changes in your work reality.

For information on publications, workshops, podcasts, and seminars by Dr. Eleniak, or to place an order, please see www.mentoringstore.ca.

I hope that you enjoyed this journey and that it has somehow made a difference for you. I would love to hear from you. If you wish to share your experience reading this book, please contact:

The Mentoring Store
North Vancouver, British Columbia
Canada V7J 2L1
1-604-988-5689
Email: info@mentoringstore.ca

About the Author

Duanita G. Eleniak, PhD, is a is a registered clinical social worker, a registered art therapist, a philosopher of consciousness studies, an educator and a published author. She is the Director of the Masters in Clinical Psychology Art Therapy program at the Adler University, Vancouver BC Canada campus. Through her private practice, 'Creative Counseling and Education', she provides individual, couple, family and group counseling. She teaches at various institutions in the Pacific Northwest and provides supervision, mentoring and consultation to other professionals. Her books, courses, podcasts and blog are available through her online mentoring services at www.mentoringstore.ca.